Gazelles in Murchison Falls area.

P.I.P. Photo by Tomas D. W. Friedmann

THE **Congo**

RIVER INTO CENTRAL AFRICA

The wake of a boat traveling along the beautiful banks of the Congo.

THE
CONGO
RIVER INTO CENTRAL AFRICA

by Patricia Lauber

Illustration by Ted Schroeder
Maps by Fred Kliem

GARRARD PUBLISHING COMPANY
CHAMPAIGN, ILLINOIS

NANCY LARRICK, ED.D.,
IS THE EDUCATIONAL ADVISER FOR THIS SERIES

The author and editor are grateful to Dr. James P. Chapin of the American Museum of Natural History for reading the manuscript and advising on its content.

The lemur, or "bush-baby," of the Congo forest, is small enough to perch on a man's finger.

Wide World Photo

Contents

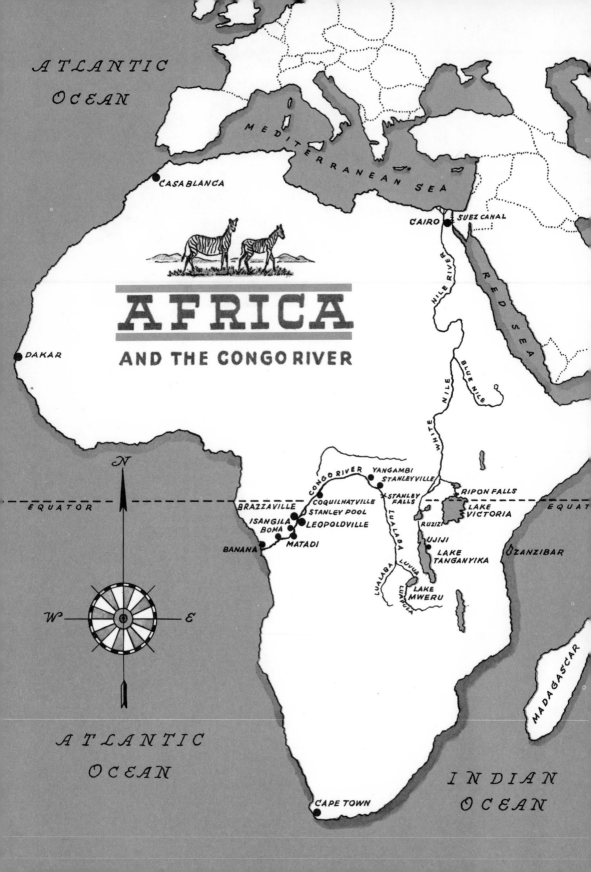

1. The Congo River

Thirty miles off the west coast of Africa, there is a brown stain in the blue Atlantic. It is the stain of land and it tells of giants—of a giant land feeding a river so big and strong that the sea cannot swallow it. The land is Central Africa, and the river is the Congo.

Every second of the day and night, the Congo pours two million cubic feet of water into the ocean. In all the world only the Amazon River has a greater flow. The Congo has carved a channel in the ocean floor. Following its channel, the river runs through the sea, carrying a huge load of mud and sand. These come from the very heart of Africa, for the Congo drains a basin nearly half the size of the United States.

The Congo and its tributaries are the circulatory system of that basin. Boats carrying passengers and freight travel their waters into an often trackless wilderness. Without this system of rivers, the young Republic of the Congo could hardly exist.

Seen from the ocean, the mouth of the Congo River has a welcoming look. Here the continent parts. The river leads the way in. The way is clear and open since the river drops its burden of mud and sand well out at sea. The mouth hides no shoals or sandbars. Its waters run deep and wide.

At the river's mouth is a slender spit of land that holds a town. The town is named Banana, although it has very few bananas. It was once a bustling slave port. Here ship after ship came in to sail away for the Americas, heavy with human cargo. Today no trace of that past remains. Banana is now a sleepy little town of coconut palms and small trim houses.

Elsewhere the river mouth is lined with beaches. There are fishing villages, with neat huts built under the palms and nets spread to dry on the sand. Among the tall palms are squat, fat-limbed baobab trees. They are strange trees with bulbous trunks, rootlike branches, and fruit that looks like long, swollen boxing gloves. Old men use their reddish bark fibers to make fishing nets.

Baobab trees and fruit.

The shore also holds a modern resort hotel, where people vacation from the hot damp areas that lie inland. The glittering water in which they swim is salt to the taste. It rises and falls with the tides. Yet it is as much the river as the sea, blackened with the mud of the Congo basin.

Sometimes manatees are caught here, where the river and sea mingle. These are the sea

The manatee, sometimes called the sea cow, has a long body and flattened tail. Its front fins are paddle-shaped.

P.I.P. Photo by Radio Times Hulton Picture Library

mammals that sailors of old mistook for mermaids. Along the banks of the river another interesting creature is seen—the climbing fish. Small and popeyed, these fish climb nimbly over the mangrove roots and are the color of mud.

The mouth of the Congo River was discovered in 1482 by a Portuguese explorer named Diego Cão. Other Portuguese followed him. Slavers raided the coast. Missionaries made converts to Christianity in the native kingdoms of the Kongo, as the region was called. Diego Cão himself came back twice. On his third trip he sailed 92 miles up the river. It was a long trip for a clumsy ship of sail, working against the river's current. Today the trip takes five hours in a fast motorboat. But what the traveler sees is not greatly different from what Diego Cão saw.

Clearly, this is a giant among rivers. It is dotted with big islands. Its widespread banks appear to be part of the horizon. At first, nothing can be seen beyond them, for they are overhung with tall, thick trees and masses of green

A native in his handmade pirogue.   P.I.P. Photo by Radio Times Hulton Picture Library

creepers. Later, the trees draw back and the land along the river's edge becomes open and grassy. Near the banks, native fishermen pole their pirogues—slender canoes hollowed out of tree trunks.

Above the present-day town of Boma, 50 miles from the mouth, the river changes. Unhurried waters give way to strong currents and whirlpools. The outstretched arms of the banks

12

tighten and narrow on the river. Thirty miles farther upstream ships must pass Devil's Cauldron, a seething, boiling mass of water. Beyond the cauldron is the town of Matadi, journey's end. Ocean-going ships, motorboats, pirogues, can travel no farther. Matadi lies at the foot of a series of cataracts. For 200 miles above Matadi the Congo plunges sharply toward the sea. Its total drop is 800 feet—five times the height of Niagara Falls.

Today a railroad and a road bypass the cataracts, linking two parts of the river. But

Matadi is the main port of the Republic of the Congo.

for a very long time there was no way around the cataracts.

Here Diego Cão was forced to turn back in his voyage. During his brief stop, he pressed on a little by foot and reached the first cataract above Matadi. On a block of hard, dark rock he carved an inscription that can still be seen today. It shows the coat of arms of the king of Portugal and the names of Diego Cão and his companions.

The rock marked the end of Diego Cão's exploration of the Congo. And for more than 300 years it marked the limit of European knowledge about the river.

During that time European explorers discovered and mapped the Americas, China and Australia. They charted the earth's oceans and major land masses. But they did little more than touch the edges of Africa. Its vast heart remained unknown.

The reason lay in the very geography of the continent. Much of Africa is built like a

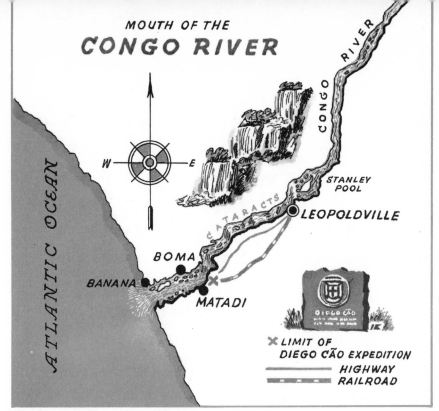

CONGO RIVER

ATLANTIC OCEAN

W E

STANLEY POOL

CATARACTS

LEOPOLDVILLE

BOMA

BANANA

MATADI

DIEGO CÃO

✕ LIMIT OF
DIEGO CÃO EXPEDITION
━━━━━ HIGHWAY
▬▬▬▬▬ RAILROAD

Early European exploration of the Congo reached only a short distance inland.

fortress. The center of it is a high plateau. Near the coasts the plateau sheers off and drops sharply in rocky walls. Rambling rivers of the plateau suddenly change to angry torrents as they dash toward the sea over a series of cataracts.

On other continents, rivers were the roads that explorers followed from the sea through the wilderness. In most of Africa they were barriers. River mouths led only to fortress walls. There cataracts blocked the way. In Central Africa rivers were not even roads to walk beside. Dense jungles choked their banks. So for more than 300 years the Congo was recognized as one of the world's mightiest rivers. But where it came from no one knew. Central Africa remained a blank on the map.

In the fortress of Africa there was only one open door—the valley of the Nile. For 1,500 miles men could follow the Nile south into Africa. Then its course was lost in a swamp the size of England. The sources of the Nile lay somewhere south of that swamp in a part of Africa that was unmapped.

Since the time of the ancient Greeks, the sources of the Nile had been one of the great mysteries of geography. By the middle 1800's the mystery was still unsolved, but a new attack was being made on it. And it was this search for the sources of the Nile that led directly to the exploration of the Congo River.

2. The Blank on the Map

In 1856 two English explorers, Richard Burton and John Hanning Speke, set out together to discover the sources of the Nile. The sources were a mystery that had fascinated geographers for more than 2,000 years. For the Nile was much more than a river. It was the life of Egypt. Year after year, without cease, its great brown waters poured through the parched desert, making life possible. Yet no one knew where it came from.

All attempts to follow the Nile to its source had failed. Most of them foundered in the huge swamp called the Sudd, where waterways were choked by floating islands of rotting shrubs and grasses. A few Arab traders had managed to get through the Sudd, but that was as far as they could go. Beyond it they faced 80 miles of cataracts.

Burton and Speke therefore decided on a different approach. They would not go up the Nile. Rather, they would sail down the east coast of Africa to the Arab island of Zanzibar. From there they would cross to the mainland, march inland, and look for the sources of the Nile in a part of Africa that was blank on the map. With this expedition the great age of Central African exploration began.

Nine years and several expeditions later, the mystery was still far from solved.

On the 1856 expedition, Speke had made a side trip by himself. He had discovered a huge body of water, now called Lake Victoria. Speke

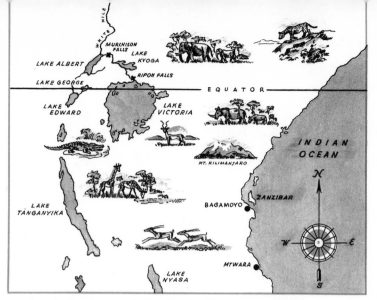

The route of Burton and Speke in their search for the source of the Nile.

immediately decided that this was the source of the Nile. Burton was outraged. Speke's lake was unknown and unmapped. Speke had not traveled around it. He did not know that the Nile flowed out of it. He did not know that *any* river flowed out of it. Burton himself favored another big lake, Lake Tanganyika, as the source of .the Nile. It was known to have a river, the Ruzizi, at its northern end. Arab traders said the river flowed into, not out of, the lake. But Burton thought they might be wrong. Arab traders were interested in slaves and ivory, not geography.

19

In 1862, Speke returned to Central Africa with James Grant. He again found a large lake. A river flowed out of it over a waterfall, which Speke named Ripon Falls. Now Speke was certain he was right about the source of the Nile. But to Burton, Speke was still the same reckless guesser. How did Speke know this was the same lake he had seen before? How did he know that the river flowing out of it was the Nile? Had he followed the river? No!

Further exploration only added confusion. And so, in 1865, the Royal Geographical Society sent out Britain's most famous African explorer. This was Dr. David Livingstone, who had first gone out to Africa as a medical missionary.

In March, 1866, Livingstone landed on the east coast of Africa, accompanied by a small caravan of porters. His plan was to head for the unexplored country south of Lake Tanganyika. He hoped to find the true source of the Nile in high mountains that fed the lake. Livingstone set out—and vanished into unmapped Africa.

David Livingstone

Three years later no one knew where Livingstone was or what he was doing. At this point the publisher of the *New York Herald* decided that there was a story in the missing Dr. Livingstone. It was a decision that later had a far-reaching effect on both the exploration of Central Africa and its history. He summoned a young reporter named Henry Morton Stanley and said, "I wish you to attend the opening of the Suez Canal and then proceed up the Nile. Send us detailed descriptions of everything likely to interest American tourists. Then go to Jerusalem,

21

Constantinople, the Crimea, the Caspian Sea, through Persia as far as India. After that you can start looking around for Livingstone. If he is dead, bring back every possible proof of his death."

Stanley carried out his other assignments and arrived in Zanzibar in January, 1871. He bought six tons of supplies and hired 157 porters. On February 18 he set out on a march that took him through swamps, over mountains, and through dense forests. He was attacked with spears and arrows by tribes that had learned to fear strangers because of the Arab slave traders. Eight months after setting out, Stanley arrived at his destination, the village of Ujiji, on the shores of Lake Tanganyika. Here Livingstone was believed to have his base. And here Stanley found Livingstone.

During his four-month stay with Livingstone, Stanley learned about the doctor's wanderings of the past six years. Early in his march, Livingstone had lost nearly all his porters and

"This engraving, for which I supplied the material, represents my meeting with Dr. Livingstone at Ujiji, Lake Tanganyika; and is as correct as if the scene had been photographed."—STANLEY

pack animals. His medicine chest had been stolen. He had been sick time and again. He lacked supplies of any kind by the time Stanley found him.

Even so, Livingstone had managed to carry out part of his plan. He had struggled around the southern end of Lake Tanganyika without finding anything that could possibly be the source of the Nile. However, continuing west, he had discovered a great river, the Lualaba, which flowed north. And so he had begun to wonder whether the Lualaba might be the Nile.

While Stanley was there, he and Livingstone went up to the head of Lake Tanganyika and the Ruzizi River. They discovered that the Arab traders were right. The Ruzizi flowed into the lake; it could not be the Nile. Livingstone then returned to the idea that the Lualaba was the Nile. There were times when he suspected that it might turn out to be the Congo River. But he had set his heart on its being the Nile, and he was determined to follow it to the sea.

To do that he needed both supplies and porters. Stanley left Livingstone some supplies and promised to send what was needed from Zanzibar. He left, carrying Livingstone's journals and his own notes. They were published first as articles in his newspaper, then as a book, *How I Found Livingstone*, which rocketed Stanley into fame.

Livingstone's years in the jungle finally affected his health.

25

Meanwhile, Livingstone had set out again with the supplies and porters sent by Stanley. But his health was poor and he died on May 1, 1873, without discovering the source of the Nile.

However, Stanley was now determined to return to Africa, finish the doctor's work, and fill in the blank on the map. It was a most ambitious program, but Stanley was a most unusual man.

Stanley photographed in the clothes he wore when he met Livingstone. His native gun-bearer is with him.

3. Henry Morton Stanley

The exploration of Central Africa is full of strange twists and contradictions. The explorers sent out by the Royal Geographical Society were soldiers and missionaries. But the greatest explorer of all turned out to be Stanley, a journalist who first went to Africa to get a story. He got his story by finding Britain's most famous explorer, the missing Dr. Livingstone. Inspired by Livingstone, Stanley went back to Africa. And so it was Stanley who followed the Lualaba River and showed it to be the Congo.

But then, Stanley himself was full of strange twists and contradictions. To begin with, his real name was not Henry Morton Stanley, but John Rowlands. And he was not American by birth, but Welsh.

He was born in 1841 of a poor family in Wales. Although baptized John Rowlands, he never knew his father. His mother did not want him and as a small child he was shunted from relative to relative. When he was six, his family boarded him out in a workhouse for poor boys and orphans. Here beatings and hunger were daily fare. At fifteen he ran away, soon signed on a ship as a cabin boy, and worked his way across the Atlantic. At New Orleans he left the ship and had the first stroke of good luck in his life. A kindly American named Stanley adopted him and gave him the name Henry Morton Stanley.

When war broke out, Stanley first joined the Confederate Army. Captured, he was sent to a prison in Chicago. He won his freedom by volunteering for the Union Army. After the war he served for a time in the United States Navy. Then he traveled all over the West as a member of an army expedition that was putting down the Indians by force.

During his travels Stanley had begun to write and soon showed himself a brilliant journalist. He was hired by the *Herald*, distinguished himself at foreign reporting, and was sent to find Livingstone. He was 30 years old when he made the march to Ujiji. He was 33 when he went back to Africa to take up Livingstone's explorations.

Unlike other explorers, Stanley did not go to Africa to reform anyone. He was not drawn back by the country itself. He did not even care

Ripon Falls was discovered and named by John Hanning Speke.
Uganda Government Ministry of Information, Broadcasting & Tourism

deeply about geography. Stanley went out to do a job. He did it with skill and efficiency, for he was quick, intelligent, ambitious and hard-working. He was self-made and determined to succeed. His methods of carrying a job through were often ruthless and they took a high toll in human lives. But Stanley was also very determined and very brave. Life had taught him to depend on himself alone. An explorer who knew him later wrote: "Stanley is a man remarkable for strength of character, resolution, promptness of thought, and iron will. . . . Difficulties do not deter him, disasters do not dismay him. . . ."

In deciding to return to Africa, Stanley had set himself three goals.

1. He would sail around Lake Victoria and find out whether it was one lake, as Speke had said, or several small lakes, as current maps showed it. He would determine whether the stream at Ripon Falls was the only outlet.

2. He would test Richard Burton's theory the

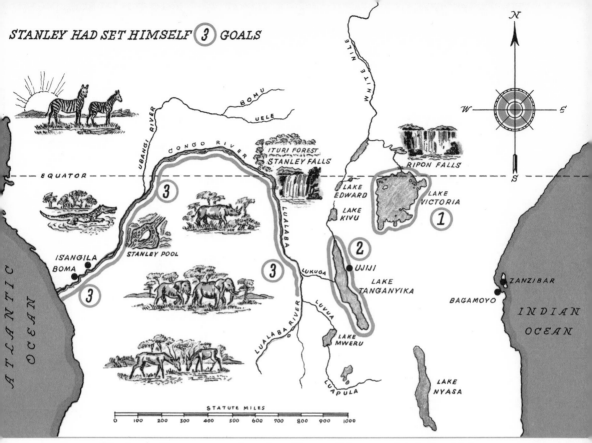

Stanley's three areas of exploration on his second trip to Africa.

same way by sailing around Lake Tanganyika.

3. He would take up Livingstone's work on the Lualaba and follow the river wherever it led.

As a first step, Stanley won backing from the *New York Herald* and the *London Daily Telegraph*. They would pay for his expedition. Next he set himself to learn all that was known about East and Central Africa. He bought 130

31

books on his subject, read them carefully, and took notes. Finally, he hired three assistants. One was a young hotel clerk named Frederick Barker, who yearned to go to Africa. The other two were brothers, Francis and Edward Pocock. They were the sons of a fisherman and were to supply boating skills. In August, 1874, Stanley and his companions sailed for East Africa.

By November they were setting out from Zanzibar. Their caravan numbered 356 people, including the wives and children of some of the porters. Among the supplies were goods for trade with native tribes. In his book, *Through the Dark Continent*, Stanley tells us that the goods included "great bales of unbleached cottons, striped and colored fabrics, handkerchiefs and red caps, bags of blue, green, red, white, and amber-colored beads small and large, round and oval, and coils upon coils of thick brass wire."

The porters were also carrying a boat, the *Lady Alice*, built in England to Stanley's design. Made of Spanish cedar, it was 40 feet long, 6

The LADY ALICE *was specially built so that it could be carried in sections.*

feet across at its widest point, and 30 inches deep. For ease in carrying, the boat could be taken apart into sections.

The expedition reached Lake Victoria in three and a half months. By this time the group was much smaller. Edward Pocock had died of typhus. A hundred of the men had been lost.

Lake Victoria from its southern shore.

Some had deserted; others had died of sickness or in battles with hostile tribes.

They arrived at the southern shore of Lake Victoria, near the spot where Speke had first glimpsed the lake and guessed that it was the source of the Nile. Stanley was not a guesser. With eleven picked Africans, he set out in the *Lady Alice*, leaving the rest of the expedition behind. Fifty-seven days later, after a voyage of 1,000 miles, he was back. The first of his three goals had been achieved. Victoria was one big lake—Speke had been right. Only one big river flowed into the lake. Only one flowed out, the river at Ripon Falls.

In July, 1875, Stanley set out for Lake Tanganyika. He had lost more men through desertion and illness. One was Frederick Barker, who had fallen sick with a chill and died. But by spring of 1876 Stanley was back at Ujiji on Lake Tanganyika. He completed his trip around the lake and found no outlet that could possibly be the source of the Nile. Burton was wrong.

Later explorers traced the Nile from Ripon Falls. But Stanley had established the main point. He had mapped the lakes and shown that only Victoria could be the source of the Nile.

Now there remained the third goal—the Lualaba River. What was it? Where did it flow?

By this time Stanley had been gone from the coast for two years. His expedition was down to half its original size. But he was not a man to turn back. In August he set out for the Lualaba and for what was to become one of the great African adventure stories.

4. "Difficulties Do Not Deter Him"

It was mid-October, 1876, when Stanley first saw the Lualaba. He tells us in *Through the Dark Continent* that it was "a broad river of pale gray color." It was dotted with small green islands. And it reminded Stanley of the Mississippi before the Missouri pours in its rusty brown waters. He says: "A secret rapture filled my soul as I gazed upon the majestic stream. The great mystery that for all these centuries Nature kept hidden away from the world of science was waiting to be solved . . . and now before me lay the superb river itself! My task was to follow it to the Ocean." And follow it he did, though he met with every possible disaster—disease, hunger, shipwrecks, and attacks by hostile tribes.

Shortly after he arrived at the Lualaba, Stanley had a meeting with a man known as Tippoo Tib, an Arab slave trader. He was eager to find out from Tippoo Tib what difficulties lay ahead in a journey down the Lualaba. And he wanted Tippoo Tib to join the expedition. The slave trader had a few hundred fighting men armed with rifles, who would greatly strengthen the expedition.

At first Tippoo Tib refused to join Stanley. "If you white men are desirous of throwing away your lives," he said, "it is no reason we Arabs should. We travel little by little to get ivory and slaves, and are years about it . . . . but you white men look only for rivers and lakes and mountains, and you spend your lives for no reason and to no purpose." Tippoo Tib also had an unstated reason for refusing. This was that he wanted to hold Stanley back. He did not want Europeans in a region that was promising for slave traders.

But greed was also strong in Tippoo Tib. When Stanley offered him $5,000 to accompany the expedition for 60 days, he accepted.

In late October they set out, Stanley and his group, Tippoo Tib and some 400 followers. It was impossible to travel on the Lualaba. Rapids and waterfalls closed great stretches of the river. The huge expedition cut overland through dreadful country. On November 6, Stanley tells us, they entered "the dreaded black and chill forest called Mitamba . . . bidding farewell to sunshine and brightness . . . the trees kept shedding their dew upon us like rain in great round drops. Every leaf seemed weeping. Down the boles and

Tippoo Tib, Arab slave trader.

branches, creepers and vegetable cords, the moisture trickled and fell on us. Overhead the wide-spreading branches . . . absolutely shut out daylight . . . we marched in twilight. . . . The path soon became a stiff clayey paste. . . ."

Soaked with dew and sweat, they clambered in and out of stream beds. The boat sections were dreadful burdens for the porters. Stanley records that these had to be driven like blunted plows through dense forest growths. He had a path cleared with axes, but the boat porters still could not march more than six miles a day. The going was so hard underfoot that in ten days Stanley wore out his shoes and had to draw his last pair from supplies.

The party spent November 16 burrowing on all fours through a tangle of branches and stems. At day's end, Tippoo Tib announced that he would go no farther. Argument and an offer of more money finally persuaded him to continue.

On they went through dense forests inhabited by leopards, elephants, large vipers and cobras. They climbed ridges and crossed ravines. From time to time they met native tribes. From the bones around their cooking pots, Stanley judged them to be cannibals.

On November 19 they arrived again at the Lualaba. Here the river was 1,200 yards wide. As they camped beside it, Stanley had the idea of building canoes so that they could follow the

The forests of the Congo are solid tangles of branches.

river as a road. Tippoo Tib considered the idea rash. There were dangerous cataracts ahead. And men in canoes on the open river would make easy targets for the warlike tribes along the banks.

Stanley launched the *Lady Alice* anyway. He and one group set sail in the boat. The rest followed by land. The going grew worse and worse. Smallpox and other illnesses had broken out among the land party. Thorns tore their feet and legs; sores formed that would not heal. They were attacked by hostile tribes.

Along the way Stanley found six abandoned canoes. He had them lashed together to form a floating hospital. Later he found a huge, damaged canoe. Repaired, it became a hospital for 60 of the sick and injured.

Some of the riverbank tribes proved friendly. Stanley was able to trade beads and cloth for food, which was fortunate since Tippoo Tib's huge following was draining his food supplies. Other tribes, however, fled at the sight of the expedition. Still others attacked with beating drums, war-horns and yells.

On December 18 they came to the island of Mpika and landed to eat breakfast. The inhabitants at once gathered, blew war-horns and mustered a large party for attack. However, before the attack could get started, Stanley managed to make peace and explained that they were only travelers going down the river.

They continued another ten miles. Then, Stanley says, "While rowing down, close to the left bank, we were suddenly surprised by hearing a cry from one of the guards of the hospital canoes, and, turning round, saw an arrow fixed in his chest. The next instant, looking towards the banks, we saw the forms of many men in the jungle, and several arrows flew past my head. . . ."

Rowing hard, they pulled ashore at a cleared area. Stanley sent out ten scouts to lie in wait in the jungle. He mustered the 30 healthy men to build a fence of brushwood. As they worked a shriek of agony rang out from one of the scouts. A rifle cracked. War-horns and yells answered. Stanley sent out 20 men to help the scouts. The remaining men finished building the tall, dense fences of brush. When the camp was ready, the recall was sounded. The scouts arrived on the run, calling, "Prepare! Prepare! They are coming!"

"Again and again the savages hurled themselves upon our stockade. . . ."

"About 50 yards of ground outside our camp had been cleared," Stanley writes, "which, upon the retreat of the scouts who had been keeping them in check, was soon filled by hundreds of savages, who pressed upon us from all sides but the river. . . . Again and again the savages hurled themselves upon our stockade, launching spear after spear with deadly force into the camp. . . . Sometimes the muzzles of our guns almost touched their breasts. The shrieks, cries

. . . the rattling volleys of musketry, the boom-
ing war-horns, the yells . . . the groans and
screams of the women and children in the hospital camp, made together such a medley of
hideous noises as can never be effaced from my
memory. For two hours this desperate conflict
lasted. . . . At dusk the enemy retreated. . . ."

Through the night the horns ˙ blew and
occasional poisoned arrows flew into the camp.
In the morning Stanley had himself rowed out

onto the river. He saw a village downstream, found it empty, and seized it. The men fortified it and there they stood off the next attack. The enemy retreated to the jungle, where they blew their horns and kept up a cry of "bo-bo-bo-bo." This was a war strain, which the expedition was to hear time and again during its journey.

"At noon," Stanley continues, "a large flotilla of canoes was observed ascending the river close to the left bank, manned by such a dense mass of men that any number between five and eight hundred would be within the mark. We watched them very carefully until they had ascended the river about half a mile above us, when, taking advantage of the current, they bore down towards us, blowing their war-horns and drumming vigorously. At the same moment . . . war-horns responded from the forest, and I had scarcely time to order every man to look out when the battle-tempest of arrows broke upon us from the woods."

They withstood the attack. And then the

advance guard of Tippoo Tib's land party arrived. The enemy withdrew. That night Stanley and a small group of men counterattacked. They rowed up the river, cut loose the enemy's canoes and towed them away. By morning most of the tribesmen had fled. Stanley informed the remainder that unless they made peace he would keep their canoes and occupy their main town. So peace was made.

Tippoo Tib, however, had had enough. He spent Christmas with Stanley and prepared to turn back. On December 28 Stanley embarked 149 men, women and children in the boat and canoes. They continued down the Lualaba alone.

5. "Disasters Do Not Dismay Him"

When Stanley parted from Tippoo Tib, the Lualaba was still flowing north. It could have been the Nile or, for that matter, the Niger. But Stanley now felt sure that it was the Congo. In high spirits he showed Frank Pocock the chart of Central Africa and promised him that they would fill in the blanks. He predicted that another four months would bring them down the Congo to the Atlantic. As it happened, he was four months off—it took eight months and in that time 33 Africans and young Frank died.

As 1876 drew to a close, however, the expedition was sailing down the Lualaba, passing points where various tributaries flowed in. They cried out, "Sennenneh!" (Peace!) to tribesmen on the banks. Sometimes the tribesmen were friendly. They made peace and sold food for goods. Sometimes they were not friendly. The expedition was attacked by one tribe whose cries meant, "Meat! Meat! Ah! Ha! We shall have plenty of meat." With the sound of "Bo-bo-bo-bo! Bo-bo-bo-bo!" ringing in their ears, Stanley and the rest of the "meat" got past and went on. There

Stanley's route in seeking to trace the Congo, a trip which took 999 days.

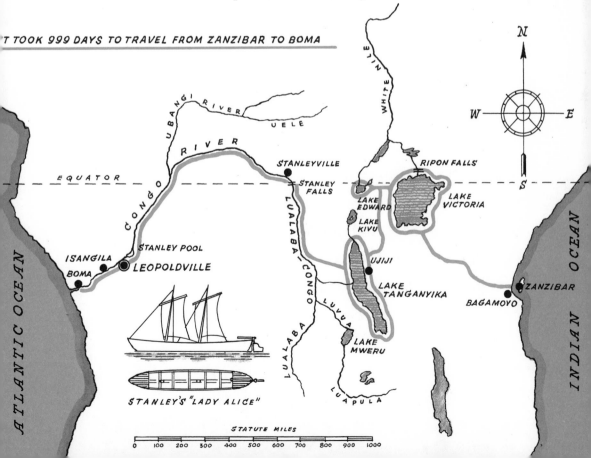

were drownings in a storm, when the river took its toll. There was illness. But on they went, crying, "Sennenneh!" One friendly tribe warned them of what lay ahead: cataracts and cannibals. They were urged to turn back. On they went.

Soon they found themselves trapped between the two dangers. Ahead they could hear the sound of the terrible falls that they had been warned against. Behind them were huge canoes filled with cannibals in war paint—bodies painted half red and half white with broad black stripes.

What should they do? Turn and face the cannibals or slide on to certain destruction? They dropped anchor and fought. Having beaten off the attack, they landed and built a stockade. When the enemy retreated, the expedition continued cautiously down the river. Shortly they came to the first of the seven terrifying cataracts that are today called Stanley Falls. Here the river narrows and hurls itself against a cliff. As it rushes on toward the falls, whirlpools snatch and swallow anything afloat.

50

One of the most beautiful sights on the Congo is Stanley Falls.

The expedition shifted to the land. For three weeks they hacked their way through the jungle, carrying their boats and supplies and fighting off hostile tribes. From time to time the river opened up and they could travel by water. But another cataract always sent them back to the land.

The river was still following a northerly course. Stanley was beginning to wonder whether it could possibly be the Congo. Surely the Congo would be flowing west by this time. While he was beset by doubts, he woke one morning to find that an unfriendly tribe had netted them. Huge fishing nets had been stretched across an open part of the river, blocking their way. They cut and fought their way free.

On January 28, 1877, they finally found themselves clear of the cataracts. Ahead lay open water. Stanley records, "We are once again afloat upon a magnificent stream, whose broad and gray-green waters woo us with its mystery." Though he could not know it, a thousand miles of open river now lay ahead. It is a trip that today takes five days. It took Stanley's group nearly a month and a half.

Stanley was soon heartened to observe that the river was definitely beginning to flow westward. About the same time he noted that so far they had survived 28 "desperate combats" and that of the whole group only 30 persons had not been wounded. However, food supplies were running very short.

They were fortunate to meet a tribe that neither ran away nor attacked them. With calls of "Sennenneh!" the boats advanced toward the tribe. Stanley stood in the bow of the *Lady Alice*. In one hand he held a banana. In the other he held colored beads, brass wire and copper bracelets. He clashed the bracelets and showed the beads. Then he lifted the banana to his open mouth. Again and again he repeated the dumb show. Finally, an old chief nodded. He had understood that they wished to trade goods for food and he agreed.

Crocodile entering the Congo.

It was the happiest of meetings. A ceremony joined the tribe and the expedition in blood brotherhood. Stanley drew on the vocabulary of native words that he had been recording. He managed to make the chief understand that he wanted to know the name of the river. The chief said, "Ikutu ya Kongo!" Now it was certain that the westward-flowing river was indeed the Congo. Here, too, Stanley found some ancient Portuguese guns. He was delighted, for this proved that they were approaching a European settlement.

54

They sailed on, wending their way around
islands, losing the river in side channels, finding
it again and continuing. The islands and banks
were solid masses of green—trees, vines, creepers.
Stanley's notes are studded with the names of
animals that he saw—elephants, baboons, long-
tailed monkeys, lemurs, hippos, crocodiles, storks,
sandpipers, geese, ducks, kingfishers. Clouds of
mosquitoes filled his tent by night and the rise
and fall of their humming kept him awake.

An elephant bathes in the river.

In March they came to a big lake in the river, now called Stanley Pool. In one way, the worst of the journey lay behind them. They knew where they were and where they were going. There was no longer any danger of being attacked; the tribes were peaceful and used to trade. And only 300 miles lay between the expedition and the sea. But in another way this last stretch proved to be one of the worst in the whole voyage.

At Stanley Pool the Congo nears the edge of the African plateau. The plateau is rimmed here by the Crystal Mountains. There is just one opening—a narrow hole drilled through the mountains by the river. All the waters gathered by the Congo and its tributaries plunge through this opening in a headlong rush to the sea. As the plateau drops off, the river boils down a steep bed filled with jagged reefs, snags of rough, hard rock and lines of boulders. Cataract follows cataract—the same cataracts that blocked exploration of the Congo from its mouth.

56

This old engraving shows Stanley's party shooting the rapids.

Stanley's expedition began the descent. Where boats could not pass, they hacked trails out of the jungle and traveled overland. Where the river was free of rapids, they launched their boats again, listening for the thunder that warned of the next drop. At one of these cataracts, three of the canoes failed to pull ashore in time. They were swept over the cataract. Only two of the men survived.

57

In the district of Inkisi the expedition was brought to a halt. Here the river flowed through a deep gorge only 400 yards wide. Forced into this narrow space, the huge river hurled itself furiously at the cliff walls and curled into towering waves. There was no question of taking the boats through the gorge. Yet on land the way was blocked by soaring, forested cliffs that leveled out on top into a tableland.

Stanley climbed to the top to survey the situation. He could see no way around the cliffs. Yet he could not take to the river and he could not stay where he was. Only one course of action remained. He climbed down the cliffs and announced his decision: They would hack a road out of the cliffs and drag their boats up.

To everyone but Stanley, the job seemed impossible. Yet somehow they managed. By the end the men were showing signs of weakness. Many were ill and all were exhausted. But food was so short that they could not stop. Stanley drove them on. However, he was deeply concerned to learn that more cataracts lay ahead of them.

In early June, Frank Pocock drowned when his boat was swamped. His death was a terrible blow to Stanley and it seemed to drain the men of their will to continue. Stanley rallied them and pressed on. In the next 30 days they progressed only three miles and there were more

Stanley had to haul his canoes around Inkisi Falls.

drownings. At one rapid Stanley himself almost drowned.

On July 30, at Isangila, Stanley learned that the sea was only five days away but that there were more cataracts in the river. He took the advice of a friendly tribe and decided to march overland. The boats were drawn up on the banks and left. Stanley led a straggling column of men toward the sea. Hunger was now their main problem. Because of nearby European settlements, the tribes had all the goods they wanted. They would not trade food for what Stanley carried. The expedition had to do without.

Finally Stanley was able to persuade a villager to carry a letter to the town of Boma, near the mouth of the Congo. Here, he knew, there were Portuguese traders. In the letter Stanley explained where he was, that he had with him 115 men, women and children whom he had led from Zanzibar, and that they were nearly starving. He asked for help. To his letter he added a P.S.: "You may not know me by name; therefore I add, I am the person that discovered Livingstone in 1871."

A letter came back and supplies followed. There was food for all the expedition and a special box for Stanley. It contained, among other things, bread, butter, tea, coffee, sugar, sardines, salmon, plum pudding and three kinds of jam.

Well fed for the first time in months, the expedition marched on. They reached Boma on August 9, 1877. After a brief rest they pushed on to the Atlantic. It had taken Stanley exactly 999 days to accomplish the three goals he had set himself.

Now his first thoughts were for the faithful survivors of the long trek. He made arrangements to take care of the sick. Then he accompanied the whole group by ship back to their home in Zanzibar.

Continuing on to England himself, Stanley began to develop a great plan that he wanted Britain to undertake.

6. The Opening of the Congo

In tracing the Lualaba and Congo rivers, Stanley had filled in a large blank on the map. And he had traveled through a vast region of unexplored resources. Certainly there was ivory to be had in the jungles and rain forests, for the tribes collected elephant tusks. Probably the forests held many other riches.

At present the region was a trackless wilderness of gloomy forests. But through the heart of this darkness ran the bright ribbon of the Congo River. The river offered a way in. If the cataracts below Stanley Pool could be bypassed, the Congo and its tributaries would open up Central Africa. In Stanley's mind the bypass

The Congo was a rich source of ivory from elephant tusks.

was the key to the treasurehouse. Without it all the wealth of the forests was worth nothing.

Stanley's plan called for bypassing the cataracts first with a road and then with a rail line. Next, he thought, trading stations should be built along the river from its mouth to its source. These would serve as collecting points for the riches of the forests, which could then be shipped to the Atlantic. Here, too, tribesmen would be paid for their work and friendly contacts built between Africans and Europeans.

Like other men of his time, Stanley believed that the coming of white men could bring nothing but good to the African peoples. For white men would teach European ways to the Africans. He did not think of African cultures as being worth saving. It did not occur to him that African ways might be better suited to the country than European ways. He did not even dream that the Africans might be shown the worst, not the best, of the white man's ways. Rather, he imagined European ideas of happiness and virtue replacing ignorance and superstition. He imagined Africans and Europeans working side by side for the good of all. And this, he felt sure, would come about through the bypassing of the cataracts and the opening of trade.

Stanley wanted Britain to take over the huge region he had discovered. To his disappointment, Britain was not interested. So Stanley turned to a man who was very interested indeed. This was King Leopold II of Belgium.

Leopold was a German prince who had become King of the Belgians in 1865. He ruled a country that was young and small and that had no colonies. Belgium was not wealthy and neither was Leopold. However, Leopold was ambitious and energetic. He was a keen man of business, and Africa interested him greatly. Fascinated by the stories that explorers brought back, he saw in Africa a means of satisfying his desire for wealth.

Leopold sent for Stanley. Together they pored over maps and talked about Africa. Finally a decision was reached. Leopold would form an international committee to pay for exploring and developing the Congo basin. Stanley would go back to Africa and direct the work.

On August 15, 1879, Stanley arrived at the mouth of the Congo. He immediately set about his most important task: building a road around the cataracts. He went up the river as far as steamers could travel. On foot he began exploring the rugged hills and ravines until he decided what route the road must take. Then the slow dogged labor of road building began.

Stanley had a work force of nearly 300 Africans, for all work was done by hand. Axes were used to fell trees, shovels to dig. Sledge hammers and drills were the tools for cutting through solid rock. The workmen had never known that rock could be shattered. So, hammer in hand, Stanley showed them how to do it—and won his African nickname, Bula Matari, breaker of rocks.

Inch by inch, foot by foot, the road was driven

forward. They worked in the muggy heat of tropical Africa and lived on beans, goat milk, and bananas. At the end of a year, they had built 52 miles of road.

The work went on. The road lengthened and lengthened and lengthened. At last it reached Stanley Pool. Here Stanley established the trading station that in time became the city of Leopoldville.

A steamboat was hauled in sections over the road and assembled at Stanley Pool. A paddlewheeler, it was the first powered boat ever to sail in these waters. Its arrival meant that the

LE STANLEY *was the first paddlewheeler to sail above Stanley Pool on the Congo.*

Atlantic and Central Africa had been linked.

Stanley moved on to the next task, visiting the tribal chiefs who lived along the Congo and its main tributaries. He was persuading them to sign a treaty of trust. It guaranteed tribesmen the right to hunt, fish, travel, trade and live on their lands. It guaranteed European traders the right to travel in peace. In all, Stanley made more than 400 such treaties with tribal chiefs.

By 1885 Stanley had finished his job. A road led around the cataracts. There were trading stations along the river. The chiefs had signed the treaties. But that year an international meeting was held in Berlin. Its purpose was to settle quarrels among European countries concerning Africa. An astounding action was taken at the meeting. The whole Congo was given to Leopold. It was not given to Leopold, King of the Belgians. It was given to Leopold as a private citizen. The region was named the Congo Free State.

Although he never visited it, Leopold ruled the

Free State from 1885 to 1908. There are different points of view about what happened in the Free State during those years, but terrible stories spread about some of the European traders who had gone to the Congo for ivory and rubber. In the United States and Great Britain it was believed that the Congo people were being stripped of their rights, used as slave labor and brutally abused. At length, world opinion was such that the Belgian parliament took over the Free State. It was made a Belgian colony, called the Belgian Congo.

In 1960 Belgium granted independence to its colony, and the Republic of the Congo was established. But the growth of the colony between 1908 and 1960 is another story. Our story is that of the river.

The river had been opened up. And this in turn opened up the whole Congo basin. Today we know that Stanley was right about its riches. The basin is a vast treasurehouse. And the giant Congo River is the key to its door.

7. The River and Its Riches

Seen on a map, the Congo River is, as Joseph Conrad wrote in *Heart of Darkness*, "an immense snake uncoiled, with its head in the sea, its body at rest curving afar over a vast country, and its tail lost in the depths of the land."

Everything about the river is big.

It is the fifth longest river in the world.

There are places where it is eight or nine miles wide.

Its waters hold more than 4,000 islands.

The Congo, its tributaries and lakes offer more than 8,000 miles of water highways. From Stanley Falls to Stanley Pool there is a 1,000-mile run without one natural barrier.

A native gathers coconuts from his unusual "ladder."

The basin drained by the river is huge. The Congo begins in eastern Africa as two other rivers. One is the Luapula, which rises in a swamp in Northern Rhodesia and flows northwest to Lake Mweru. It flows out of the lake's northern end as the Luvua River. The second

71

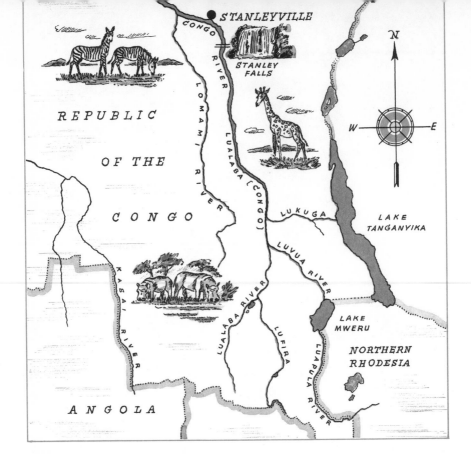

river is the Lualaba. Flowing north, it meets the Luvua. Where the two join, the Congo really begins. However, the river goes on being called the Lualaba until it crosses the equator near Stanley Falls. Then it swings west in a wide arc and flows toward the Atlantic, crossing the equator once more on the way. Together the Congo and Lualaba rivers stretch 3,000 miles through Central Africa. Their many tributaries

72

fan out north and south for thousands of more miles. All told, the Congo basin is the size of the United States east of the Mississippi. Most of it lies within the Republic of the Congo.

The amount of water carried by the Congo River is enormous. Its discharge is the second largest in the world. And the flow is steady the year round. Unlike most rivers, the Congo does not have a dry season that makes navigation impossible.

The reason for this great and steady flow of water has to do with the Congo's course. The river runs through the part of Africa that receives the most rain (up to 90 inches a year). It also winds along the equator—it is the only major river in the world whose main stream flows through both the Northern and the Southern Hemispheres. As a result, it benefits from both rainy seasons. It is fed by the April-to-October rainy season of the Northern Hemisphere. From October to April it is fed by the rainy season of the Southern Hemisphere.

P.I.P. Photo by Tomas D. W. Friedmann

The southern part of the Congo basin is good country for lions.

However, the basin is not all tropical rain forest. The southern part, for example, is high, rolling land that receives much less rain. This land is covered with tall grasses, while trees grow chiefly along the banks of streams. The grass and leaves are food for buffaloes, antelopes, elephants, zebras and gazelles. The tall grass provides cover for the lions, leopards and other beasts of prey that stalk grass- and leaf-eating animals.

74

The okapi is one of the Congo's rarest animals.

Elephants, the source of the ivory that drew both Arabs and Europeans into the Congo, also live in the rain forests. So do monkeys, apes, wild hogs and one of the Congo's rarest and shyest animals, the okapi. The okapi is a close relative of the giraffe, but it looks more like a long-necked, purple-brown horse with white stripes on its rump and legs.

The animal life of the forests is endlessly varied. There are golden wildcats that live by clawing fish out of the rivers. There are dormice with tufted tails. Among the many kinds of snakes are a number of tree climbers. Parrots chatter by day, while large, fruit-eating bats wing across the rivers by night and call loudly as they hang in trees.

Insects abound in the heat and damp. Mosquitoes and gnats buzz in clouds. There are tsetse flies, bees, wasps, beetles, brilliantly colored butterflies and dragonflies, centipedes and spiders. Driver ants march in long columns. The so-called white ants, which are really termites, build nests that may tower 20 feet high.

The river waters have many inhabitants. Crocodiles sun themselves on sandbars. Nearby a shiny dark rock turns out to be the gleaming broad back of a hippopotamus. About a thousand species of fishes live in the rivers. Among them is the Nile perch, which may weigh well over 200 pounds, and an electric catfish that can produce a shock strong enough to be felt through a leather sole. There are fresh-water herring, elephant-snout fish, barbel, spiny eel and tigerfish that weigh 100 pounds.

In spite of the many rivers, fishing is not a commercial industry. Crocodiles make it a dangerous occupation. And, in any case, fish are not easy to ship in tropical heat. Some tribes fish for their own needs, but that is about all.

The basin's hot, damp forests hold a rich store of plant life. Here the lowest branches of the big trees may be 60 feet above the ground. Beneath the big trees grow smaller trees.

Lazy-looking hippos sun themselves in the river.   Annan Photo Features

Scattered through the forests are hardwoods like mahogany and ebony. There are rubber trees and kapok trees and hundreds of other kinds. Tall palms sway along riverbanks. And the banks, like the islands, may be masses of bright flowers whose perfume hangs heavy in the air.

Travel through the rain forests is in some ways just what it was in Stanley's time. The traveler is bitten by insects, scolded by monkeys and made sodden by the same wet heat. Let him step off a path or road and he will have to fight his way through the same undergrowth that tore the feet and legs of Stanley's men.

Today, of course, there are railroads as well as many new roads suitable for automobiles. But it is almost impossible to cross the Congo basin by road or rail. To travel any distance, one must fly or go by river. Since flying is expensive, most traveling is done on the rivers.

Some of the riverboats are big, modern ships with diesel engines. Others are paddle-wheelers, known as "packapacks" because of the sound the

A paddle-wheeler pushes barges on the Congo.

paddles make slapping the water. Paddle-wheelers are well suited to river travel. They do not draw much water and they can be eased in to shore at places where there is no dock. A big riverboat seldom travels alone. Usually it is pushing an extra boat for third-class passengers and several barges piled high with freight.

The freight traveling the Congo River gives some idea of the region's industries and resources. Boats service the republic's 13,000 factories, which make, among other things, bricks, cement, tiles, paint, fertilizers, candy and clothing. They supply the textile mills. They carry coffee, tea and rubber from plantations to processing plants. Downstream to the Atlantic go the Congo's most important agricultural exports: coffee, palm oil, cotton, rubber, timber, cocoa, tea, peanuts and manioc, a starchy root that is a food staple.

However, the chief treasure of the Congo lies buried in the ground. The Congo has a vast belt

Congo paddle-wheelers are fueled with wood. Natives all along the river gather wood in piles on the banks.

Quentin Keynes from Gendreau, N. Y.

Katanga provides the raw materials for Congo industry.

of copper in Katanga Province. It has tin, gold, cobalt, zinc, manganese, platinum, chromium and other ores. It produces 60 per cent of the free world's industrial diamonds. Geologists think there may also be oil, methane gas and bauxite (the raw material of aluminum).

Katanga used to produce most of the world's radium and more than half of its uranium. (The uranium for the United States's first atomic bombs came from Katanga and traveled down the Congo River.) But these deposits are now used up.

Tapping mineral wealth requires electrical power so that ores can be refined into metals. In Katanga hydro-electric plants have been built on rivers. Elsewhere in the republic most electricity is produced by heat—through plants that burn wood or coal. But the amount of power that the rivers could produce is fantastic. The cataracts below Stanley Pool could produce 114 million horsepower. That is one and a half times as much as all the rivers in North America could produce. The entire Congo basin probably contains one-fourth of the world's waterpower.

And so the Congo and its tributaries are themselves a gigantic natural resource.

To date very little of their power has been harnessed. Big hydro-electric plants are expensive to build. There is no point in building them unless their power is needed. However, small plants are being built on the tributaries, for as changes come to the Congo, the need for power grows. Electricity is needed for homes, businesses, streets and factories. It is needed at mines, plantations, lumber camps and refineries. It is needed on farms and in village workshops.

As the country develops, the Congo River system will play a double role. It will supply power to mines, factories and plantations. And it will carry away their products to the sea. Doing so, it will bring more and more changes into the lives of its people.

8. People of the Congo River

Rivers, like roads, are bearers of change. New ideas and new ways spread along them, always touching the lives of the people and sometimes changing them greatly.

When the Congo River was first opened up, it brought terrible changes into the lives of its people. Earlier, over a 300-year period, European and Arab slave traders had stripped the region of millions of people. The Congo Free State cost still more lives.

Today the Congo basin has a population of about 13 million. Most of these people are Bantus. They are black or brown Africans who resemble

Negroes but, strictly speaking, are not true Negroes. The Bantu race developed long ago when a light-skinned people called the Hamites moved south and began to intermarry with the Negroes. Today the Bantus are divided into some 200 tribes, and they are spread all over the Congo basin.

A traveler along the Congo is struck by the mixture of old and new. On a road outside Stanleyville are three men carrying bows and arrows as naturally as Europeans carry umbrellas. They are passed on the road by a big American car taking local politicians to a town meeting. The meeting is attended by men in business suits and by chiefs in furs, feathers and leopard skins.

A road running out of Stanleyville leads through the Ituri Forest, following a route once taken by Arab slave and ivory traders. The Ituri Forest, which takes its name from a river that becomes one of the Congo's main tributaries, is the land of the Pygmies.

The Pygmies are a dwarf people who average

The Ituri Pygmies hunt with bows and arrows.

less than four and a half feet in height. Well muscled and alert, they move swiftly and silently through their forest home. They are wanderers who live in hunting bands. They seldom leave the forest for long. Out of its shade and shadows they get sunstroke. Used to clean forest water and to mosquitoes and flies that do not carry germs, they have no resistance to the germs of the outside world. And so they are a group threatened by modern changes that shrink the forest.

Upstream a little from Stanleyville is a village of mud huts. This is the home of the Wagenia fishermen, who still fish the rapids in the way that Stanley described. In big pirogues the Wagenia cross the wild waters to hang fish traps from logs and vines strung above the rapids. Fish swimming downstream are caught in the traps. On a return trip the fishermen bring in their catch by climbing up the vines to the logs. Balancing themselves above the rock-studded waters, they pull up their traps.

The Wagenia fishermen use fish traps made of vines.

The native market in the center of Stanleyville is a busy place.

Stanleyville itself is a brisk, modern frontier town, set in the forest. Built on both sides of the river, it is an important port. All shipping coming upstream must stop at Stanleyville. The way beyond is blocked by the rapids of Stanley Falls.

From Stanleyville it is an easy five-day run downstream to Leopoldville. The diesel-powered boat churns away from its pier, pushing the extra passenger boat and its barges. Within minutes Stanleyville is left behind. Carried by the current, the boat caravan moves smoothly down the river.

At Yangambi is a big agricultural research station built by the Belgians. Nearby is the village of the Topoke. They launch their pirogues and paddle out to sell fruit and vegetables to the passengers. As they near the steamboat, it is easy to see that they still follow the old tribal custom of tattooing their skins with raised scars.

The modern boat churns on; the Topoke turn back. Now there is nothing to be seen but the forest, what Conrad described as "Trees, trees, millions of trees, massive, immense, running up high. . . ." Giant kapoks tower above the mahogany and palm trees. A sudden tropical shower hoses the river, the forest and the boats. When it ends, the fresh-washed green shimmers in the sun.

At Coquilhatville the boat caravan docks. This is a small, modern town, with its main street running along the equator. Some cargo is unloaded; new cargo is taken on. The trip continues. From time to time the caravan stops to discharge passengers or cargo at a refinery, a plantation, or a mission. In some places pirogues act as water taxis. At others a plank is lowered. If it doesn't reach the bank, passengers wade ashore. At each stop village women hawk meat, fish, vegetables and fruit from baskets carried on their heads, for many of the third-class passengers do their own cooking. A crew member buys a small crocodile, cuts it up and sells the meat, which tastes like chicken.

Even where the forest is thickest, the marks of men can be seen. A tiny clearing marks a Bantu village. The houses are almost invisible, for they are made of what the forest and river offer—saplings as poles, vines, reeds, clay, palm leaves woven into roof mats. They are designed to let air circulate and to shed rain.

A patch of different green marks the garden. Here women and girls grow bananas, yams, manioc, corn, beans, or other crops. The men are hunters or fishermen.

The villagers take care of their own needs. They make pirogues by chopping and chiseling out the centers of big logs. They weave baskets. They make nets out of vines. They pound the soft inner bark of wild fig trees into cloth. Palm

Bantu huts are made of materials handy in the Congo.

nuts supply oil for cooking. A village amuses itself at night with music from drums, flutes, a stringed bow and other homemade instruments.

The forest is a strange and often frightening place to those who live in it. And so witch doctors and medicine men are powerful figures. It is their job to control the spirits and the elements. Yet the hand of change is also reaching into the villages. As the steamboat draws nearer, a dark speck turns out to be a man riding a bicycle along a slippery path.

The river stretches on ahead, a bright line cleaving the dark forest. No bridge crosses it. No road runs beside it for more than a few miles. Yet there is life all along its banks. Pirogues appear seemingly from nowhere to tie up beside the caravan while their owners sell food to the passengers.

On the fifth day, the caravan reaches Stanley Pool. Two cities come into sight. One is Leopoldville, the other Brazzaville. Leopoldville, once capital of the Belgian Congo, is now capital

Leopoldville is one of Africa's few large cities.

of the Republic of the Congo. Brazzaville, once capital of a colony called the French Congo, is now capital of yet another Congo Republic. At Stanley Pool the Congo divides the Congo from the Congo.

Leopoldville is one of the few real cities in Africa, with a population of more than 300,000. It has a ten-story skyscraper, air-conditioning, banks, a big sports stadium, broad streets lined with shops, warehouses stacked along the river, an airport with one of the longest landing strips in the world, a daily newspaper and two radio stations.

A few miles outside the city is the young University of Lovanium. It has more than 800 students, a big faculty, a teaching hospital on campus and a nuclear reactor.

While the Congo was a Belgian colony, many Congolese were trained as carpenters, crane operators, railroad engineers, accountants, clerks, laboratory technicians and so on. Now, because of this new university and one outside Elizabethville, the Congo is graduating its first professional people—doctors, dentists, architects, civil engineers, scientists and lawyers. They are people who have come a long way from the warriors and fishermen that Stanley met less than a hundred years ago on his long voyage down the Congo River.

Today a new Africa builds along that river. But to the river itself there is no old and no new. It carries new and old alike and reflects, as it has always done, the life along its banks.

Index

Meet the Author

PATRICIA LAUBER reports that she has been writing ever since she was taught how to use pencil and paper and that she never wanted to be anything except a writer. After being graduated from Wellesley College she went to work in New York, where she became editor of a magazine for young people and was later the editor-in-chief of *Science World*.

During these years she also kept writing and is now the author of more than 30 books for young people. Some of these are fiction, chiefly humorous animal stories. Some are science books. And others concern some of the many regions she has visited in the United States, Canada, Europe and the West Indies.

At present, besides writing books, Miss Lauber is senior science editor of a young people's encyclopedia. She lives and works in New York City most of the year. She is the author of *The Mississippi: Giant at Work*, also in the Rivers of the World Series.

Blue wildebeests, or gnus, and calf.

P.I.P. Photo by Tomas D. W. Friedmann